DIRECTING
ON CAMERA

A Checklist of Video and Film Technique

Harris Watts

AAVO

First published in 1992 by Aavo Media
8 Edis Street London NW1 8LG UK

ISBN - 0 - 9507582 - 2 - 1
British Library Cataloguing-in-Publication Data.
A catalogue record for this book is available from the British Library.

Illustrated by Bryan Reading
Typeset by Dick Hammett
Cover design by Fran Newman
Printed by A.L.Print Works

For

Christina, Jon, Matthew, Lucy and Amy.

Thanks

to Paul Watson, David Heycock, Robin Gwyn, Larry Toft, Garry Boon, Michael Kennedy and Jon Watts for corrections and suggestions.

The author

Harris Watts has worked in television since 1965 as a producer/director, first in current affairs and then in science programmes for both the BBC and ITV. From 1977 to 1979 he was Programme Production Manager in Brunei and since then he has worked in training, mainly in the UK as a Senior Instructor with the BBC's Television Training department but also abroad. In 1982 he published *On Camera*, followed by a series of *On Camera* training tapes, which collected six awards in the UK, US and Australia. *Directing On Camera* is his second book.

Note

Everything in this book applies to both video and film, unless indicated to the contrary. I often use 'film' to stand for both; writing 'video or film' each time would be tedious. 'Edit' and 'cut' are also used interchangeably. I have tried to include the feminine form of roles and pronouns often enough, I hope, to reflect the balance of sexes in the programme-making world.

PLAN

SHOOT FOR EDITING

EDIT

INTERVIEWS

SHOOT FOR VIEWERS

PLAN

Programmes are a shared experience

What is a good programme?

The best answer I can think of is a programme that offers the viewer an experience: entertaining, enlightening or (at the very least) diverting. The more moving the experience, the better: interesting, amusing, funny, fascinating, alarming, thrilling, mind-blowing, extraordinary, total—anything but boring. The test is: do people talk about your programme the next day?

'Did you see that programme about...?' 'Yes, wasn't it...?'

Any comment (other than condemnation) and you have scored. You have shared an experience with the viewer. The intensity of the experience measures the success.

The way to make a good programme is to plan. The best programmes look effortless; they seem to have fallen into place.

The best programmes conceal their art

You can't think of a way of changing them, they feel right, they just are. But don't be fooled: their art is to conceal their art. Their strengths come not from good luck, but from hard work and planning. Luck comes into it, but luck follows hard work and planning—it's not a substitute for them.

So the first thing you have to do when you are making your programme is plan.

Show things happening

Television is moving pictures. So it's no use turning up to shoot when the meeting is over, the factory is empty or the children have gone home. Whenever possible you should shoot action, not inaction. There's no point filling the screen with nothing happening—it doesn't offer much of an experience for the viewer to share. You need to show things happening.

Suppose you are going to make a short film about houseboats. What are you going to shoot? If your answer is 'Houseboats' and nothing else, you haven't done enough planning. A collection of shots of houseboats might make a photographic exhibition, but it won't make a film. Your viewers need something less static, something with a bit more movement.

'But there's nothing happening here...'

First impressions of locations are often less than encouraging. Spend some time on the location. Stop and look and think and ask questions. What is the daily routine of the person living on the houseboat? What are the advantages and disadvantages of houseboat living? How do you look for a houseboat if you want to buy one? How did the owner find this one? What interests you about the boat and owner? What about the neighbours and the surroundings—anyone or anything interesting there? If you are chatting to someone later about your visit, what do you talk about? The answers to these questions will give you ideas for happenings to shoot.

The happenings don't have to be grand or important. The houseboat owner showing the camera (and the viewer) round his boat (kitchen, bathroom, bedroom and so on); the houseboat owner fishing from the deck (one of the advantages of living on a boat); the houseboat owner locking up and setting the burglar alarm (one of the disadvantages of living on a boat), perhaps explaining points and answering questions from an interviewer as he does so. It begins to feel like a film.

Of course it's often difficult to show things happening. Events don't arrange themselves for the convenience of the camera but unhelpfully take place on difficult-to-reach locations, at awkward or unpredictable times, are dangerous or too long drawn out to shoot. Or they don't suggest pictures or can't be seen. Or they don't happen when you visit because the people stop whatever they are doing to talk to you. What would they be doing if you weren't there?

Many events can't be seen

Or there are no happenings. This is the challenge of the 'exhibition' film, which sets out to interest viewers in a collection of paintings/statues/prints/stamps/cars/stone-age tools or what-have-you. The problem is that all the subjects of the exhibition film are inanimate. Nothing moves—if anything did, you would probably have to stop shooting!

So what do you do with exhibitions? Static wide shots of static displays are extremely boring. Close-ups are better (at least the viewers can see the exhibits) but there still isn't much happening. Zooming and panning introduce some camera movement but don't help much unless viewers can see some point for them. You need someone talking, but if he or she just talks about the exhibits one by one, you end up with a talking catalogue, not a film. The only way to make the exhibition film work is to get some intellectual action into it (see 'Find an angle' below). The speaker needs to talk to some purpose; you may then find that intellectual development begins to make up for the lack of physical happenings.

Generally speaking, however, viewers like to see happenings, not hear people talk about them. Events on screen offer a more direct experience for viewers to share than reports of events. Occasionally an exceptional speaker is so engrossing or an interviewee so moving that the talk itself becomes a happening. But this is rare. Don't rely too much on talk; look for happenings to shoot first.

Find an 'angle'

This isn't an invitation to slant the story. It's a plea for you to think of a way of telling the story that makes it mean something to the viewer. Facts alone are not enough—you aren't preparing an encyclopedia entry. You have to find a point of view from which to tell the story. Without a point of view or angle a story invites the criticism: 'So what?' Remember: 'Programmes are shared experience'. A 'so-what?' story leaves the viewer cold and uninvolved.

Finding an angle can be difficult; experienced programme-makers often spend a great deal of time agonizing 'how to do the story'. There are usually remarkably few things that you must tell the viewers; programmes don't have a long compulsory agenda like instruction manuals. Television is bad at delivering masses of detailed facts; viewers can't take them in. It's also slow; 30 minutes of TV news will fit on to the front page of a broadsheet paper and has about the same number of stories. So you have to select what you want to put across.

It may help to put yourself into someone else's shoes and look at the subject of the film from his or her point of view. The exhibition film I mentioned above (finding an angle is another of its problems) could be approached from the point of view of the artist, the exhibition organiser, the critic, the historian, local artists working in the same medium, the attendants guarding the exhibition or members of the public visiting (or not visiting) the exhibition. Or the subject of the exhibition may suggest a more original approach.

The important point is to work really hard at finding a good way to tell your story, as this will shape the programme. For one thing it will suggest—and this is a great bonus—what is worth shooting and what isn't.

Think in sequences

When you are planning a shoot, think in sequences, not single shots. A sequence is a visual paragraph, a group of shots recording an event or sharing an idea in the finished film. A shot is to a sequence as a sentence is to a paragraph.

When you start planning a film you don't need to think about individual shots, any more than you need to think about individual sentences when you are preparing to write—shots and sentences are too detailed at this stage. Sequences are more appropriate blocks to handle. They will stop your thoughts getting trapped in a bog of detail. I have often seen beginners starting to plan a film like this:

'Let's see. I'll start with a long shot of the street and pan on to the houseboats. Then I'll cut to a close-up of the letter-box and a hand will take out the letters—no, I'll do a mid-shot of the owner coming out to collect his post—no, a close-up first of the door opening, then a mid-shot of the owner...'

At this stage, the shots don't matter. The important point is the idea for the start of the film: houseboat owner emerges to collect post. How you cover it—one shot or many—comes later.

Then identify key moments

The problem with most sequences is there's too much happening. The trick then is to identify the key moments. Which parts of the action matter? Which are irrelevant?

Take the sequence above, the houseboat owner collecting the post. You might think that too little happens, not too much: 'Not exactly spoilt for choice, am I?' you murmur.

But think again. Look at some of the details. The door to the cabin (the houseboat's front door): how is it fastened? Is there a doorknob? A lock? Several locks? Or perhaps one or more bolts? Is the door mounted on hinges or does it lift off like the hatch on a sailing boat? Does the owner walk out or are there steps out of the cabin? What is he wearing when he emerges? Where is the letter-box and what sort is it? How is it opened? There is a letter in the box. Do you want the viewers to see the address? What about the contents?

You can see that even a simple sequence like this offers a wealth of details. Which are the key ones? The answer, of course, depends on the story you want to tell. If security is a nightmare on houseboats, then the locks and bolts are important. If the owner is getting old and houseboat living is becoming a bore, then the cabin steps may be relevant. If the location of the houseboat is important or the letter announces that mother is coming to visit, then the address and the contents of the letter are worth showing to the viewer.

It's up to you to decide which are the key moments. You may decide you don't want to go into too much detail at this stage of the film and need only establish this person on this houseboat—fine. The point is there is a huge number of ways of treating the opening sequence and the way you choose to do it depends on what you want to say.

Identifying key moments concentrates the mind. It also suggests how to shoot the sequence. If a detail is important you have to make sure the viewer sees it. The reason for the shot will then suggest to you where to put the camera and what the size of shot should be.

Often when the action is longer and more complicated, picking the key moments is the only way you can cover the event. On these occasions you have to identify the parts that stand for the whole, the highlights that convey the essentials. Think of the key moments (almost too familiar) at a wedding: *Here comes the bride,* 'I will', the ring, leaving the church, cutting the cake. The key moments in a manufacturing process or laboratory test or houseboat owner's morning routine are more difficult to find, but they always exist.

Keep a notebook

Your notebook should be the history of your film. For longer films it's vital, but even for shorter films you will find you need to make a surprising number of notes.

Start a notebook on the first day of research and keep it with you as you talk, visit, view, read and think about your subject. Telephone numbers, lists of things to do, ideas for shots and sequences, useful phrases for the commentary or narration, questions you must remember to ask interviewees, points from books and films you have researched—jot them all down in your notebook. Let it grow with the film. Read through it periodically to check that you are making the most of your material.

Do a treatment or storyboard or shot list

So far you have been researching and making notes. Now it's time to get things down on paper. There are various methods.

The *treatment* is best for longer films—anything over about five minutes. It offers you a vantage point: a view of the land ahead and a chance to plan your route across it.

<u>TREATMENT: JACK AND JILL</u>   *1*

Girl stops car to pick up boy (see storyboard)	
library film: cartoon sequence from 'Some Other Life' showing Jack & Jill	*SOF: nursery rhyme & music*
children tumbling on Greenwich Hill	*COMM: J & J - shorthand for boy meets girl for centuries; eg <u>Midsummer Night's Dream</u> 'Jack shall have Jill, Naught shall go ill'*
woodcut for first printing showing 2 boys	*So why does this 1765 woodcut show two boys?*

To do a treatment put a list of the picture sequences on the left of the paper and a note about the sound on the right: sync sound, voice-over, music or effects. If you then do an estimate of how long each sequence will last in the finished film, you can see if you have planned enough material. You should always plan to shoot at least 10 per cent more than you will need for your target duration so that you can drop the weaker material during editing.

Storyboards make you think pictures. If this is your weak point, a storyboard is worth doing for this reason alone.

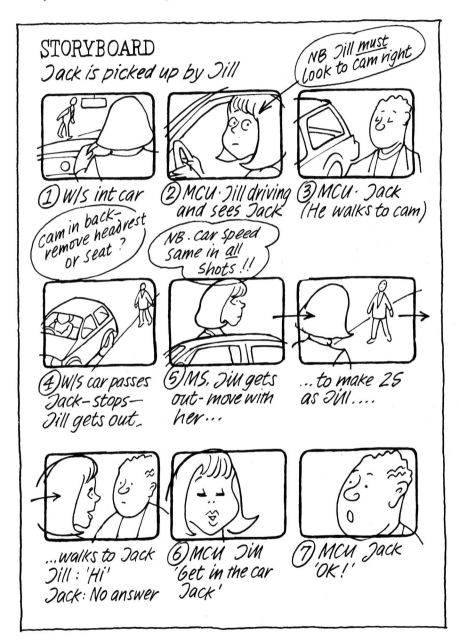

You usually need only one drawing per shot. If it's a developing shot (Jill walks along the pavement to meet Jack), draw more pictures to cover the shot or draw the key moment only (obviously, in this example, the point when Jill meets Jack). Don't worry if you can't draw: storyboards work well with just pin men or sausage men (a small fat sausage for the head, a big sausage for the body, three sausages for each arm and leg). Write a short description of the action (Jill walks to Jack) and a note about the sound (Jill: 'Hi!' Jack: no answer) under each picture. You can also jot reminders to yourself for when you are shooting (car speed same in all car shots!).

The third method is to write out a *shot list*. This works best for short films that you don't have time—or don't want—to storyboard.

SHOT LIST: JACK AND JILL OPENING

1   w/s interior car from back seat. Jill is driving through leafy suburban street. She/we spot Jack on the pavement walking the same way

2   interior shot from nearside back of Jill driving, passing Jack, stopping and leaving car

3   MCU Jack notices car slowing

4   w/s car passes Jack, stops and Jill gets out

5   MS (across car roof): Jill's head appears over roof as she gets out. Move with her as she goes round back of car to make 2s fav. Jack as Jill walks to him. Jill: 'Hi!' Jack: no answer.

(w/s = wide shot MCU = medium close-up MS = mid shot
2s fav. = two-shot favouring...)

Even for longer films that already have a treatment, it is a good idea to shot list or storyboard individual sequences the night before you shoot them. There are two reasons for this. Firstly, because the shot list or storyboard makes you think pictures.

You may have done the treatment several weeks before and forgotten—or not bothered—to think down to the level of individual shots. And secondly, because you can use the shot list to work out how much time you will have for each shot.

To work out the time per shot, start by working out how much time you need for travel to the location, for meals and other breaks. Allow at least 20 minutes for unpacking and setting up on location, and 20 minutes for clearing up after the shoot; if you are using lights, allow at least 30 minutes at both ends. Subtract this total from your working day and divide the remaining time by the number of shots on your shot list. This gives you the maximum number of minutes per shot—I say maximum because you will be lucky if anything takes less time than you planned for it.

It's difficult to say how long you will need for each shot. It depends on what you are shooting, whether you are using lights and how fast you can work. But 6-7 minutes per shot is good going. If you are using lights, 10 minutes per shot is very good going. If during the planning your minutes-per-shot number gives you less time than this, decide which shots or sequences you can drop. But do this before the shoot; you can't afford the time during it!

Don't let all this planning, however, make you inflexible. Shooting the film will throw up problems you haven't planned for, problems you will have to sort out on the spot. It will also throw up opportunities—and these you need to grasp with both hands.

Is this interesting?

When you have put your film on paper (as a treatment, storyboard or shot list) stand back for a moment and ask yourself: is this interesting? Would you watch it as a viewer? Give an honest answer.

If the answer is no, try to work out what is wrong. If you can identify the mistakes at this stage, there's still time to rethink.

Is the subject of the film interesting? Often you are asked to make a film about a subject that isn't particularly interesting. This, however, doesn't give you an excuse to be boring. You still have to find a way of making it interesting, even though this would prove that your first reaction was wrong. It's difficult to work up enthusiasm to prove oneself wrong and this reluctance (possibly unconscious) may have made you neglect some promising angles. Perhaps it's led you to spend too much time on an unfruitful part of the subject. Try a different approach, or perhaps a mix of approaches. Would any of them work better?

Perhaps the problem is not the subject but what you say about the subject. Try telling somebody some of the things you plan to say in your film. 'People live in houseboats. The houseboats are on the water'. Your listener will start looking for the nearest exit. Statements that you would never dare say to someone because they are so obvious and boring often go unchallenged on television. Some producers seem to think that normal modes of thought don't apply to the small screen and so it's OK to talk rubbish. I don't agree. If a remark is obvious and boring in real life, it's obvious and boring on television.

Perhaps the problem is not the what? (the subject or what you are saying about it) but the how? So it's not the story that is at fault but how you tell it. Perhaps your approach to the subject is too verbal: a reporter saying things to camera at the opening, interviews linked with a few general views of the location, a closing statement to camera. Talking heads and wallpaper. You aren't showing things happening but telling people about them. Think again about the points in this part of the book; then work through your shooting plan, making it more visual and less verbal. Give the viewers action, not words.

Perhaps you already have a good visual treatment but it's not in the right order. Try dropping the first two sequences of your film, or putting the ending at the beginning, or telling the story from someone else's point of view. You may have become a bit too set in your thinking. Playing around with the film in this way may re-introduce some mental flexibility and give you some new ideas.

Finally, think of the viewers. Who are they? Are you trying to appeal to too general an audience and saying too little as a result? Perhaps you should get more detail into your film. Ask yourself, does the film offer viewers who are interested in the subject an experience: entertaining, enlightening or—at the very least—diverting? This, after all, is the point of the whole exercise. You are probably going to lose those who have no interest in the subject (though aim to keep them) but if you can't satisfy those who are interested, you're in trouble.

If you aren't sure where you stand, go through your plans with someone whose judgement you respect. See what they think and listen to the questions they ask. A fresh mind can turn up a lot that you have missed. Spectators often see more of the game than the players.

Or, if you have the chance, go back to the location for another look. You may have missed something. Watch and listen. Turn round 360 degrees—the relation between the location and its setting may put things in a new perspective. What is there worth saying about the surroundings? The spirit of the place may give you an answer.

Allocate responsibilities

It used to be much easier: roles were fixed. People worked as directors, producers, director/producers, camera or sound persons, researchers or interviewers. Everyone did his or her job and responsibilities were clear.

Now the roles are less defined. Better equipment, smaller crews and multi-skilling have blurred the edges. Everyone does everything; the danger is that no one does anything very well. Directing, shooting, lighting, sound recording, interviewing and editing are distinct crafts, easy at a hum-drum level but difficult to excel at.

Don't make matters worse by blurring responsibilities as well. If no one is responsible for anything in particular, your results will be worse than they need be. If the lighting is ugly, it may be because the person who put the lights up wasn't sure whether the cameraman (or woman) was going to tell him how to adjust them. The director didn't say anything because she thought that the cameraman was looking after the lighting; anyway she was busy preparing the interview and wondering who was going to set up the mike...

It really is important that everyone should have a clear role (or clear roles) for each film. If you want to run a democratic organisation and let everyone take a turn at everything, swap roles for each film. But stick to one role (or one set of roles) per film. This doesn't mean that people shouldn't help each other and offer the occasional suggestion about something that isn't part of their job. It does mean that everyone takes responsibility for his or her job and decides how best to do it. It also means that the director has overall responsibility for the film, listening to suggestions or delegating as he or she sees fit. But he or she is the leader of the team and firmly in charge.

Good films are made by teamwork, not by committee.

Think one stage ahead

Film-making falls into distinct stages: research and planning; doing a treatment or storyboard or shot list; shooting; editing; writing narration or commentary; dubbing. Each stage prepares for the next. So you should always be thinking one stage ahead.

Planning is preparation for shooting. So when you are planning, you should be thinking about shooting. What are you going to shoot? How?

When you are shooting you should be asking yourself: 'How will it cut together?' If you suspect that the shots may not work together as intended, do an extra shot in case you need it during the edit.

In the edit room you are concentrating on making the pictures and location sound work. But you have to keep one jump ahead and think about the narration, music and effects that will be dubbed on later. You should also turn your mind to publicity:

selecting shots for a trail, writing a billing, perhaps arranging a launch.

If you don't think ahead, you will find you have to keep going back to re-plan, re-shoot and re-edit—or put up with a film that isn't as good as it could be.

SHOOT
FOR
EDITING

Shooting is collecting pictures and sound for editing

It's difficult to predict how well shots will work on screen. Shots that you have slaved over turn out rather ordinary; shots that you have taken as an afterthought turn out to say it all. How much of this shot do you need? How fast should this zoom be? It's often difficult to give the right answer when you are shooting. This difficulty with prediction is not a sign of inexperience or incompetence: Woody Allen has exactly the same problem and always films three times as many gags as necessary because he finds that jokes can be funny on paper and funny during the shoot but still fail on the screen. (See *When the Shooting Stops... the Cutting Begins* by Ralph Rosenblum and Robert Karen, published by Penguin.)

So it's dangerous to equate the shoot with the making of the film. Of course the shoot is important, very important. But it's only part of the film-making process; it's not the whole process. Film-making is very much like cooking. You choose your recipe (subject and angle), write out a shopping list (treatment or storyboard or shot list), get some money (you need more than you think) and go shopping for the raw materials (shoot the pictures and record the sound). Then you return to the kitchen (the cutting room) and start cooking (editing). The meal is made in the kitchen; the film is made in the cutting room. Shooting—like shopping—is the collecting part of the process.

So when you shoot, shoot for editing. Take your shots in a way that keeps your editing options open. This doesn't mean you should shoot everything that moves from all possible angles: that would be both wasteful and muddled. It does mean that you should plan and shoot to give yourself as wide a choice of ways of cutting as possible. This is the idea behind most of the points in this section.

Brief camera and sound

The cameraman (or woman) and sound recordist are the people you will be working with most closely at the shooting stage. You may not have met them before they arrive on location (make sure you get there first) so obviously it makes sense to start by briefing them.

The briefing should be short and to the point. Start by saying a few words about the film: what it is about, how much you have shot and the importance of today's shoot. Outline the plans for the day, answer any questions and then start on the first setup. The briefing may last only a few minutes but it is important to get it right. If you do, camera and sound will be on your side, working for the success of the film.

Two reasons why your briefing may go wrong: you don't know what you're doing, or you aren't communicating clearly. The first shouldn't happen if you have done your planning. The second is mainly a bad habit: 'Well, er, I haven't had a moment... there's been a bit of a rush on...um, problems...we'll need lots of close-ups...the story is a bit difficult to explain...oh yes, very important, we must finish by 2.30 to get to the other place to shoot the meeting.' Such bumbling is easy to cure: stick to the essentials. What, when, where, with whom, why. If you tend to be vague, jot down the important points.

After the initial briefing you also need to brief before each shot. Don't forget to include the sound recordist: too often he or she is left to eavesdrop as you talk with the cameraman. Or—worse still—is left to guess the next shot from the position of the camera. The recordist has his own set of problems and although he can be relied on to sort out most of them himself, he needs to have the information to enable him to do so (see 'Shoot sync' and 'Minimise background noise').

The people appearing in your film also need to know what is happening, but you will have discussed this with them before the shoot. You now need to tell them what they are doing for each shot. You don't, however, need to tell them what you are doing for each shot. Only professional actors (and not even all of them) like to know that the next shot will be a close- up, a pan or a focus-pull.

Remember that briefing is a two-way process. Try and be clear about what you want, but be ready also to listen. Don't ask for suggestions—a blizzard of bright ideas can waste time. But if any are offered, consider them, and don't be frightened to say no (give a reason). Or even yes.

Finally, after the shoot, if the crew has been helpful, make a point of sending a thank-you note. You might work with them again!

Shoot close-ups (use a tripod)

Television screens are measured in centimetres rather than metres. They're small. People can look like toy soldiers, houses no larger than matchboxes. On a medium-sized screen the human head is life-size only when it's in close-up.

The smallness of the average screen is one good reason for shooting close-ups: if you shoot too wide, people miss the detail. There's another reason, perhaps less obvious. Your viewers are not an audience of one or two million, but millions of audiences of one or two. They expect to be addressed individually, not en masse; the fireside chat works better than the conference speech, a glance is more effective than a theatrical gesture. Television (as someone said) is the art of the raised eye-brow. Viewers want to be face-to-face with an individual, not in the back row of the auditorium.

Most of the screen is wasted

So you need close-ups. Beginners often shoot too wide. Their eyes pick out the details of the scene they want to look at but they forget to make the camera do the same. As a result only a tiny part of the screen is showing what the director (and the viewer) wants to see. Most of the screen is wasted. Already small, the screen has been shrunk still further.

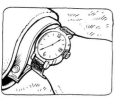

Shoot close-up!

This is not a plea to shoot everything in big close-up. That can be as uncomfortable as having someone shout in your face. But while you are shooting, check that the whole of the screen is earning its keep. Look at the monitor (if you have no monitor, look through the camera) and make sure the shot concentrates on what you want the viewers to see and excludes everything else. Tight, precise framing gives a film attack and style. Flabby, imprecise framing denotes a dull attack and no style.

Two warnings. The first is about cut-off. This is the border of the picture—about two centimetres wide—which appears on monitors and viewfinders but doesn't appear on televisions at home. As far as directors are concerned, it's a no-go area. So don't leave anything you want viewers to see at the very edge of the picture, or your close-ups of things like signs will end up as 'O PARKIN' or 'ANGER—KEEP OU'.

The second warning concerns the tripod. The tighter the shot is, the harder it is to keep steady. This is true particularly with subjects that don't move: signs are again a good example. The usual excuse for not using the tripod is '...not enough time'. It's not very convincing. Using the tripod does take a few extra seconds but this is no time at all compared to the minutes wasted dithering about on the average shoot. If you want to save time, dispensing with the tripod is not a good way to start.

There are situations when it's impractical to use a tripod—for example, when there's a crowd or a riot or you are shooting from a small boat or car. In these and other situations wobbly pictures may be unavoidable, if you don't have a specialist mount. Some people even like the wobbles, believing that they add to the immediacy of the shot. I think the argument can be overdone.

When did you last see wobbly pictures in a Hollywood feature film?

Shoot overlaps (repeat the whole action)

Many of the close-ups you shoot will be repeat actions: someone reads a letter he has taken from his pocket in long shot, then does it again in close-up.

Does what in close-up? Read the letter? Or take it from his pocket?

He should do both.

Why not shoot just the close-up of the letter with the person reading it? After all, that is the part of the close-up you are most likely to use. Fine, until you think about the cut. The cut from the long shot of the person reading to the close-up is unlikely to be brilliant—cuts between two static shots rarely are. What if (as often happens) the person holds the letter in a different way when you shoot the close-up? The cut then looks extremely unpleasant. So the close-up of the letter with the person reading it offers you just one cut, and not a very appealing one at that. If it doesn't work, the only thing you can do is abandon the close-up.

Consider the difference if you shoot overlaps—that is, repeat the complete action in the close-up: the person pulls the letter out of his pocket, takes it from the envelope, unfolds it, reads it and then, for good measure, walks out of shot. This opens up a whole range of options in the cutting room.

You can cut from the long shot to the close-up at any point. Probably the best point is to cut on the action as the letter comes out of the pocket: cutting on action is usually a better cut than cutting between two static shots. Or you can cut when the letter is being taken out of the envelope: the cut may allow you to shorten the opening of the envelope if this appears too long on the screen. Or you can cut when the letter is being unfolded: again you may welcome the chance to shorten any slow or awkward action.

You can also cut back to the long shot at any point you wish. Or you can stay with the close-up till the person walks out of shot (he can then be anywhere you want in the next shot). Or you might decide to run the whole action on the close-up (the viewers will presumably have seen your subject before and will see him again). Or you can decide, as before, to dispense with the close-up and play the scene on the long shot.

An extra bonus for shooting overlaps: your subject is more likely to hold the letter in the same way in both long shot and close-up because he has had to perform the complete action each time. If he does change his hold, cutting on the action will give you a chance to disguise the discontinuity.

Shooting overlaps gives you an infinity of choices in the cutting room. I really mean infinity, because if the complete action is accurately repeated, you can switch between long shot and close-up at any point (though some points will make better cuts than others). Overlaps are the essence of shooting for editing.

One tip: have your subject repeat the action slightly slower in the close-up. When things are bigger in the frame they appear to move faster. In fact some actions, like flicking a light switch, happen so fast in close-up that the viewer will miss them altogether if he blinks.

Start and end people out of shot

We have almost covered this one already. Remember how I suggested you shoot the complete action for the overlap: 'the person pulls the letter out of his pocket, takes it from the envelope, unfolds it, reads it and then, for good measure, walks out of shot.' The last part of the action, moving out of shot, is what concerns us here. It's another detail that increases your options in the cutting room.

What happens if the person doesn't walk out of shot? When you cut away from him reading the letter, you are probably limited to cutting to a wider shot of the same action. Cutting to a shot of him unlocking his bicycle, for example, will be a jump cut and is unlikely to look good. On the other hand, if the person walks out of shot at the end of the close-up, you can choose anything you like for your next shot: he can be unlocking his bicycle, walking down the road, sitting in a bus, lying in bed or anywhere you want him.

As a general principle, therefore, make sure the action starts out of shot at the beginning and goes out of shot at the end. For the shot of the man unlocking his bicycle, start with the bicycle (hold the shot for about ten seconds), have the man walk into shot, unlock his bicycle and then ride off out of shot.

At the end of the shot make sure the cameraman doesn't pan to follow him (unless you want the shot to last a long, long time); keep the camera still and the bicycle will soon exit. You will find

this start-and-end-out-of-shot technique gives you enormous freedom when you are cutting.

Incidentally, when you start people round the corner or just out of frame, make sure they start some way back. It takes a moment to get up speed. It's surprisingly easy to spot if a person coming round the corner has just started to walk. The same is true of a car or bicycle or runner: it's easy to see if they are accelerating when they should be cruising. If you are filming runners, make sure they pant in all the shots; they always get their breath back while you are setting up the next shot.

Shoot cutaways (look for parallel action)

An oddity about cutaways: you don't need to start and finish people out of shot. Another oddity: shoot cutaways, but try not to use them.

What are cutaways?

Shots used to avoid jump cuts.

What are jump cuts?

You are editing an interview and decide to shorten an answer. This produces a jump cut: the picture jumps because the interviewee is in a different position on the screen before and after the cut (unless you are very lucky).

SHOOT FOR EDITING

The easiest way to remove the jump is to insert a cutaway; this disguises the jump by separating the discontinuous shots. The obvious cutaway to use is a shot of the interviewer listening—hence the familiar shot of the interviewer nodding his head, known in the trade as a 'noddy'. If you see a noddy, you know the interview has been cut.

A better way to avoid the jump is to make the jump bigger: in other words, cut to a differently sized shot of the interviewee, or one taken from another angle. If the difference in angle or size is large enough, it will usually disguise the discontinuity in the picture. The reason (I think) is that if the shots are too similar, the brain assumes the action is continuous and can't help noticing the jump; if the angles or sizes are different, the brain assumes the shot has changed and concentrates on linking the subject matter instead of the composition. So too small a jump looks like a jump cut; a big jump, on the other hand, looks deliberate and works.

It's difficult to vary shot sizes and angles if—as is usual—you have only one camera and aren't in complete control of the action. It usually isn't practical, for example, to get an interviewee to do the whole interview twice so that you can shoot it again from a different angle with a different size of shot. But if you are shooting an interview and for some reason have to stop, it's worth remembering to move the camera and change shot size before continuing. If you have time at the end, repeat the parts of the interview you most expect to cut, so that you have them in two sizes and from two angles. The editing will be easier.

Remember to shoot cutaways, but try not to use them (as I said earlier). The reason is that cutaways don't advance the story; they are there purely for a technical reason (to avoid jump cuts). So they dilute the action and slow things down. Many producers think they are worse than the fault they are supposed to fix and prefer fast dissolves, wipes or jump cuts, naked and unashamed —anything, rather than a cutaway. It depends on your style and taste.

The way to make cutaways more acceptable is to make them advance the action. In an interview this would mean only using a cutaway when the interviewer does something that is worth showing—laughs or perhaps raises a quizzical eyebrow. Unfortunately the points where you want to shorten an interview aren't necessarily the points where you want to see a reaction. Most cuts will land at places that demand no reaction from the interviewer, except that you may want to remind viewers that the interviewer is still listening, which viewers expect anyway. If the interviewer's ears flapped when in use—it could even be made a condition of employment—listening shots would be much more interesting.

Away from interviews, however, it's easier to find cutaways that advance the action. You are shooting a funeral, for example. The procession takes an age to come down the road and pass the camera. In the cutting room you decide to drop the middle of the shot, so the hearse in effect jumps down the road. This edit is almost certainly unacceptable as a jump cut - the pace and style are wrong for the subject. A cutaway of weeping bystanders, however, would work well since it would disguise the jump and advance the action.

The way to test if a cutaway advances the action is to ask yourself 'Would I do this shot if I didn't need it as a cutaway?' If the answer is 'Yes', you have a more than acceptable cutaway. The way to find such shots is to look for the parallel action, preferably action more vigorous (and visual) than looking or listening. You know that you have found something really good when the action, rather than the crew, is the centre of attention.

Most actions, you will find, have a parallel, something that is going on at the same time. The parade goes by, the crowds wave; the band plays, the conductor conducts; a person travels, he has come from somewhere (or is going somewhere) where something worth showing is happening. If you shoot a sequence that will need a lot of cuts to make it work (for example, a detective looking for clues at the scene of a crime), look for the parallel action and make sure you cover it well. If you can't find a parallel action, try intercutting the sequence with something that complements it, even though it may not be strictly parallel in time or place (intercut the detective investigating the scene of crime with shots of him or her interviewing people who knew the victim).

Parallel action, of course, is the reason that the action in cutaways doesn't need to start and finish out of shot (the 'oddity' I mentioned at the beginning of this section). Shooting the parallel action already gives you the freedom you want in the cutting room.

Final thought: where's the parallel action in the one-person-alone type of film—on our houseboat, up a mountain, or on a desert island? If you film Robinson Crusoe, there won't be much parallel action to shoot before Man Friday arrives.

Do a geography shot

A geography shot shows the whole location (as much as is practical) or the location in its setting. Either way, it's a general view that establishes where you are; in fact it's often known as a general view (GV for short) or establisher.

Taking it can be a chore as you have to move the camera and equipment a little way back to get the shot. You may also have to move the film unit's cars and vans if they are cluttering the shot or it's obvious that they belong to the unit. A little foresight can save all this upheaval: park your vehicles where you know they will be out of shot. If that's not practical, do the geography shot first, before you park and unpack to start on the main action.

You should also do a geography shot for interviews though obviously you don't need to move as far back for this, just far enough for the speakers' lip movements not to be visible. You can then use the geography shot as a cutaway and lay the sound from the interview over it. Make sure that you have a generous uninterrupted measure of each person talking and listening. Make sure also that interviewer and guest take the geography shot and cutaways seriously. If they laugh and joke because they are relieved the interview is over, the cutaways may be impossible to use.

Shoot long

There's no point shooting hours and hours of tape if you have no idea how you are going to use it. That makes editing both time-consuming and expensive. Going to the opposite extreme —shooting each shot at precisely the length you think you will need and not a second longer—is also a mistake. 'You need a three second cutaway of the weeping bystanders?' (Whirr, whirr...three seconds). 'Done! Next shot?' It seems incredibly speedy and efficient on location.

When you arrive in the cutting room you realise the speed was indeed incredible. A three second shot on location won't give you three seconds of usable material. If you are working on tape, you need five seconds' run-up in case you want to overlap the sound in the edit; you may also need it to give the editing machines time to get in step with each other (if they are out of step, the picture will tremble for a moment after the cut). If you are working on film, the shot needs a moment or two to settle after the clapper board has been taken out. Furthermore, what felt like three seconds on location turns out to be two in the cutting room (you are under pressure on location so your sense of time speeds up). And anyway, you realise you need six seconds—not three—of weeping bystanders (pressure affects perception too). To get six usable seconds after the run-up you need to shoot at least ten. Fifteen seconds would be better.

'It's not long enough' is a frequent lament among editors, particularly when they are trying to cut material where the cameraman does several shots without stopping—for example, an executive at a computer followed by a close-up of the executive followed by a close-up of the computer screen followed by a close-up of the keyboard. If you are in a hurry, it's all too easy to underestimate the length needed for each part of the scene and end up with shots that are too short to use.

Shooting long is essential for editing. It also goes easily with a sensible way of working on location. If you are directing a scene, you should complete the preliminaries for each shot (asking everyone to be quiet, starting the camera and recording run-up) and then wait a moment before cueing your performers. Screaming 'Action!' at the top of your voice is not the best way to start the action; it may make you feel like a big-shot director but it rarely gets the best performance out of people. Often a calm 'In your own time...' or 'When you're ready...' works better.

At the end of the shot don't yell 'Cut!' the moment the action is over. Wait for a second or two (you may need to hold the shot in the cutting room) before giving the order. I often ask the cameraman to cut when he or she feels ready because he is in a better position to judge when the action is really over. This is particularly true for documentaries: many a revealing moment has been lost because the director has shouted 'Cut!' too soon. On-camera afterthoughts can be most rewarding in reportage.

There is never enough time on location, no matter how long the shooting schedule: two hours, two days, two weeks or two months. Save time while setting up shots, not while shooting them. Shoot long.

Be opportunistic (line up two shots at once)

When you are shooting, stand behind the camera. If you have a monitor, keep it near the camera. Behind or near the camera you can see the camera's point of view and communicate with the cameraman. You can also see what isn't in shot and perhaps ought to be.

You are doing a shot of a beautiful garden and a butterfly floats by. You are on a village green and a horse and cart rattles past. If you are near the camera, you are in the right place to ask the cameraman to go for the shot. It pays to keep your eyes open and take your opportunities.

Sometimes an interruption to a shot can be very rewarding—if you are quick enough to recognise it as a rewarding moment and not as an interruption. A child wanders into the shot while you are interviewing the mother. Don't stop. Keep running and see what happens.

If you are doing a close-up of someone hammering a tent peg into the ground and the camera is also in the right place to get a shot of the guy-rope being tightened, there's no point starting and stopping for each shot. Instead, brief the cast and crew that you would like to do both shots in one take. Then when the tent-peg shot is over, keep running while the cameraman frames up on the guy-rope. When camera and sound are ready, cue the action and the second shot goes into the bag.

The important thing in this cult of opportunism is to make sure that your crew and performers can follow you. Their contribution to the shots may be far more complicated than yours and it may not be easy for them to concentrate on two things at once, or in quick succession. In such cases don't try for two shots in one take. The director can get too clever!

SHOOT FOR EDITING

Hold shots at both ends of the zoom
(3 for the price of 1)

If you are doing a zoom—to a sign outside a building, for example—remember to hold the beginning and the end for about ten seconds each. This takes an extra 20 seconds on location but you profit in the cutting room because you now have three shots for the price of one, plus 20 seconds. You can use these shots separately, in pairs, all together (unlikely) or—as far as the static shots are concerned—in reverse order.

While you're at it, do the zoom backwards as well (pull out from the sign to show the building). Another few seconds invested, another option created for the cutting room.

Use the zoom for framing

The zoom is a seductive toy. It may be fun to use on location but the results are not much fun in the cutting room.

The best way to use the zoom is for composition. When you are setting up a shot, zoom in to cut out the dead area round the edge of the picture and fill frame with what you want the viewer to see. Or zoom out to make sure that important parts of the picture aren't lost in cut-off (the area at the edge of the picture that home television sets don't show). Or move the camera back and zoom in to benefit from the foreshortening effect at the narrow-angle end of the zoom—it can be most attractive. As an aid to composition the zoom lens is wonderful.

As a camera movement, however, it is less satisfactory. First of all, zooming is only half-good at enlivening a static picture. It may feel right to zoom when you are shooting a motionless scene or object—if only because it gives you the feeling of doing something, not just pointing the camera. But the artificial movement of the zoom won't add much interest to the picture. On the whole, boring pictures stay boring, zoom or no zoom.

Then it's difficult to know how fast to zoom. 'How long do you want it?' the cameraman will ask, once the opening and closing frames have been established. There's a big difference between —say—a three-second and a five-second zoom but it's difficult to feel the difference. Try counting while you imagine the shot. Or play safe and do one at each speed.

Then, as with most camera moves, zooms are difficult to shorten in the cutting room. If you cut when the camera is moving, the cut usually looks snatched.

Finally, too many zooms give viewers the feeling they're on the deck of a heaving ship in a storm—uncomfortable and undesirable, if not exactly lethal.

On the other hand, used carefully, zooms can be effective. In a crowd shot, for example, zoom in to highlight a particular person or group of people. Or combine the zoom with another camera move so that the shot ends perfectly framed (as the car comes up the drive, pan and zoom to end on the host anxiously waiting to greet his father-in-law-to-be). Often zooms work best when they start close (on the country cottage, for example) and then zoom out to reveal something (the monstrous electricity pylon towering above it).

But don't let zooms become a habit. Because they are easy, they easily become a substitute for finding the best way to shoot something. Use them sparingly and only when you have a good reason.

Motivate camera moves

In fact all camera moves, not just zooms, should have a good reason. A shot that drifts into a close-up of a man's tie (nothing to do with the story) or wanders off sideways to show an irrelevant antique chair (so what?) looks as if it's out of control. People stop watching the story and start wondering what's going on. There should be a caption at the bottom of the screen: 'WARNING—RUNAWAY CAMERA. NORMAL SERVICE WILL BE RESUMED AS SOON AS POSSIBLE'. Pointless camera moves draw attention to themselves. If moves have a reason, people don't look at the move, they look at the picture.

Motivating camera moves is not difficult; just let the camera follow the action. The pan and zoom to the man waiting to greet his father-in-law-to-be is so well motivated most viewers won't notice it. It's also logical for the camera to go to the tie or antique chair, if the interviewee is talking about them. (It's probably better, however, to shoot the tie and the chair as cutaways and insert them later in the cutting room in precisely the right position and at precisely the right length. This also gives you a chance to edit the speaker's words without having to worry about jump cuts.)

Keep continuity of direction (don't cross the line)

Keeping continuity of direction is a principle of film-making that you should know about. In principle you should also observe it; in practice there are occasions when you need not.

The principle is that positions and directions of movement should be consistent on screen. If a car is travelling right to left in one shot, it should continue right to left in the next—or it will appear to have turned round.

This is true of any action on screen. It should continue in the same direction (right, left, up or down) if you want the shots to make sense in a sequence.

You should keep continuity of direction also for things that don't travel. If you take two shots of an art student examining a painting in a gallery, the student should face the same way in both shots. If he faces left in the first shot and right in the next, viewers begin to wonder where the painting is. 'On the left, isn't it?' 'No—on his right.' 'But he's looking at another picture now...at least, I think so.'

There are two confusions here. The first is the problem of left and right. Whose left and right are we talking about? If I face you, my left is on your right, and vice versa. The way to avoid this confusion is always to use the camera's left and right on location and emphasise you are doing so by using the terms 'camera left' and 'camera right'. So you say things like 'Look camera left in both shots' or 'Move camera right'. Everyone then knows what you are talking about.

The second confusion comes from not knowing where to put the camera to keep continuity of direction. The way to avoid this is to imagine the shots on screen. If the art student is facing camera left in the first shot, he should face camera left in the second and you can move the camera anywhere that keeps him looking left. This approach (imagine the shot on screen) always works. It's also slightly easier than the other method, which is to work out where the 'line' (or 'axis') lies.

Think back to the car coming down the drive. The car moves left to right in the first shot. The way to keep it going the same direction in all the shots is to keep the camera on the same side of the drive. If you do this, the car can move towards the camera, across the camera or away from the camera—no matter, it will always be going left to right. The drive is in fact the 'line'. Cross the drive/line and the car will change direction on screen. Stay on the same side and the car will keep its continuity of direction on screen. It doesn't matter which side of the drive you choose to shoot from at the beginning; what you must not do is change sides while shooting the sequence.

Where is the line in the art gallery? If you don't know, work it out on a piece of paper. Draw a bird's-eye-view diagram. Place your camera so that the student is looking camera left. Then slide the camera around until he starts looking camera right. You will find the line runs through the top of the student's head and along his nose to the painting—you might call it his line of looking. Take the camera across this line and on screen he will start looking right.

With the cam on this side of the line, the art student always looks left.

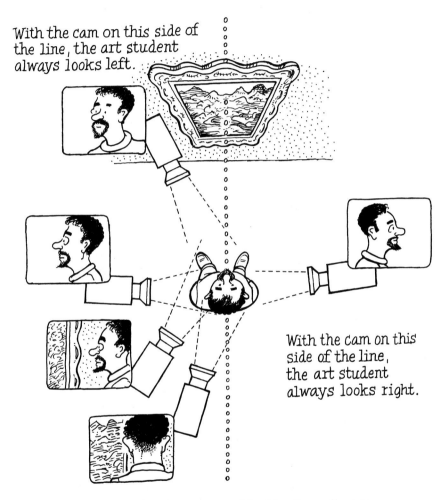

With the cam on this side of the line, the art student always looks right.

Now suppose the student is an expert hired by the gallery to advise if the painting is a forgery. You need lots of shots of him examining the picture but having him face camera left in all of them would be tedious. The way to include shots of him facing camera right without it looking like a mistake is to place the camera directly in front of or behind him. The shots from these positions are neutral as far as continuity of direction is concerned. So you can follow an in-front-of or from-behind shot in your cut sequence with a shot of the expert looking camera left or right—it doesn't matter. Every time you want to change the continuity of direction during the edit you put in a neutral shot as a buffer. The buffer shots for the car coming down the drive are the car driving straight towards camera (don't get run over) or driving directly away from camera.

If you are shooting with two cameras, the need to keep continuity of direction will dictate where you place them. At a political meeting, for example (where the line, of course, runs through the noses of platform speakers and audience), you will have to position both cameras on the same side of the hall or one at the side and one at the back. If you decide you must place cameras on both sides of the hall, be sure that you have time and opportunity to take buffer shots from the platform (difficult) and the back of the hall to allow you to cut back and forth across the line. With a long sequence it may become acceptable to cut across the line without going through a buffer shot every time, once you have established the geography. Viewers will remember that platform speakers and audiences face each other.

Keeping continuity of direction gets complicated when there is more than one line. In group discussions, courtroom scenes and round-the-table events like dinner parties, boardroom meetings and card games, the line and relative directions change every time you move the camera to show another person's point of view. The way out of this difficulty is to shoot a master shot and cut back to it whenever you need to re-establish the geography. Also cover yourself by shooting singles of people looking first one way and then the other if you aren't sure which direction will be correct.

There is also more than one line if people move across the screen together—a horseman, for example, riding escort to a lady driving a carriage. If you want to shoot close-ups from each person's point of view, one should look camera left and the other should look camera right. No problem, except that the scenery behind the carriage and the scenery behind the horseman will move in opposite directions when you cut from one close-up to the other. This happens because there are two lines in this situation: the line of travel and the line of looking. You won't be able to avoid crossing one of these lines if you want shots from both performers' points of view.

Continuity of direction will occasionally give you problems. The answer usually is to think what the shots will look like in sequence on the screen. If this doesn't work and you can't work out where the line is (or which one applies), cover yourself by doing the shot both ways. And try not to worry. In simple situations it's nice to get it right but if you are having problems, the chances are the situation isn't simple.

There are occasions, at pop concerts or at the political meeting I mentioned earlier, when it is acceptable to cut across the line, once the relationship between platform and audience is established. Generally speaking, you can get away with crossing the line if you can do it without viewers losing track of what's going on. So in the example of the car driving down the road,

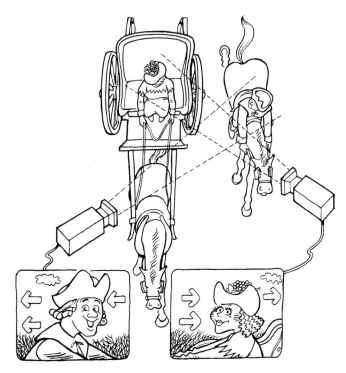

The scenery moves in opposite directions when you cut

viewers would almost certainly understand that the car had not turned round if there was no reason why it should have. Or possibly the shots were composed to show the car's speed or the locations it was driving through rather than the motion of the car. We're now into areas of taste and 'It depends on the situation...'

In the end it does depend on taste and situation—and who you are. Crossing the line is a useful convention. If you are a famous director brimming with confidence, you may consider yourself free to ignore convention. If you are a learner, you may prefer to observe it.

Shoot sync (and keep quiet)

Pictures without sound are like a meal without spices. They lack flavour and bite. They need sound to complete the experience.

Some directors think they will save time by shooting without sound. They may save a little time when they are setting up the shot because they don't need to worry about the mike. But the seconds saved on location will cost hours during the edit, spent looking for sound to fill the gaps.

Sound effects from discs are a poor substitute for the real thing. They are excellent for supplementing what has been recorded on location but building up a complete track from disc is hard work and expensive, with results that often seem undernourished. In theory you can recreate any sound you like in a dubbing theatre; in practice you end up with a few stock acoustics ('busy street', 'market', 'room', 'hall' etc.) that don't begin to match up to the infinite variety of sound in the real world.

As for synchronising all those sounds of cars, footsteps and slamming doors with the pictures, that's a problem only major prestige productions can think about tackling. Humble television programmes that don't have sync sound quickly settle —are forced to settle—for background music or generalised effects. The problem with background music is that it wastes a direct channel straight to the viewers' emotions. The problem with generalised effects is that they are no substitute for the real thing.

So it makes sense to record sound for every shot, not just for the talking heads. This means you have to give the recordist time to find the right place for the mike. You also have to keep quiet while shooting; you can't talk your performers through the action or your voice will be on the track. But even if you have to say a word or two while shooting, it's still better to shoot sync. Good sound with the occasional interruption from the director is preferable to no sound at all. Cutting an occasional directorial comment from the track is far easier than building up a track from scratch.

Minimise background noise (if wanted, dub it on later)

Of course, on some locations it's impractical to shoot sync, because of background noise.

If the noise is very loud, it may drown the sound you want viewers to hear. You will have to wait for the noise to stop, or ask for it to be stopped, or (sometimes) find a quieter location. If—like the noise of a passing aircraft—it lasts a long time, you should keep on recording until the sound has faded, even if the action finishes first. This gives you a chance to fade out the offending noise smoothly and unobtrusively during the edit or dub.

The one thing you shouldn't do is to ignore the background noise. Once it is on the recording, it is almost impossible to get rid of without damaging the sound you want to hear, even in a fully equipped dubbing theatre. Furthermore, it will sound worse on the recording than it does in real life. Our ears can to some extent select what we want to listen to in real life because the sound comes from different places. But they do less well with recordings because the source of the noise is often not on the screen and all the sound comes from the same place, the loudspeaker.

So when you are shooting, ask people to switch off air conditioners, fridges, washing machines, music, chiming clocks, vacuum cleaners—anything that is out of shot and likely to interfere with the sound you want. If you want to shoot with a TV, radio or compact disc playing in the background, shoot with the background sound turned down and record it later as a separate track (for the TV, record the sound from another set or get hold of the track later). This gives you complete freedom to cut the pictures and foreground sound as you wish. You can then dub on the background sound later.

Finally, remember that ears—like eyes—weaken with age. As a result many people have difficulty isolating words against a background of noise or music. Intrusive noise is one of the commonest complaints from viewers. Minimise background noise and a lot of people will be grateful.

Be flexible about shooting order (but watch continuity)

Films don't have to be shot in the right order, any more than newspapers have to be read in the right order. If you shoot in the order you expect to cut, you may waste time moving the camera, and even more time moving the lights. So it makes sense to finish all the shots in one lighting set-up and on one location before moving. You should sort out the shots you need from each camera position and location when you are planning the shoot.

On the other hand, don't mess around with the shooting order more than you need. Actors won't thank you for having to mix up their emotions as you mix up the scenes. Even with a documentary you may be asking for trouble if you insist on shooting the closing sequence first; the experience of making the film could modify your thinking and your ending. And continuity can become a nightmare in both drama and documentaries if you jump around too much. Think before you jump.

Check video recordings, but not too often

One of the joys of video is that you can play it back on location, immediately after taking the shot. Enjoy this privilege sparingly; don't overindulge. Too much checking wastes time and batteries. If you aren't sure whether a shot worked, it's often quicker to air your doubts, suggest improvements and then do another take.

But do remember to check your video recordings after the first shot on a new tape and after moving to a new location. With both film and video it's possible to shoot away merrily and find the stock blank. Video gets the bad news to you quicker—if you check.

Keep it simple

The catchword for this is KISS, which stands for 'keep it simple, stupid'. I don't much care for 'stupid', so I prefer to keep it simple.

Extremely complicated shots are usually more trouble than they're worth. A close-up of a young driver in the rear-view mirror. He looks left as he turns left into a driveway. The camera zooms out to show the drive and a house through the front windscreen. A young girl appears at the front door and runs towards the car. The driver jumps out of the car and runs forward to sweep her into his arms. We hear another car screech to a halt behind. The camera moves up to the rear-view mirror again and we see it's a sports car loaded with young men. They jump out and rush forward to join the embracing couple. The camera zooms out again to show the whole gang hugging and kissing.

It's a terrific opening.

But all in one shot? There are many problems. Both cars have to stop on precisely the right spot. The boy and girl have to meet on precisely the right spot. Everyone (boy, girl, cars, camera) have to get their timings precisely right: one mistake and the momentum of the sequence is lost. The shot will take ages to set up and more than a few takes to get something usable, let alone get it right. And the final problem is that when you view it in the cutting room, the shot may say more about the brilliance of the director than it does about the opening of the story.

Keep it simple. Break down the action into shots, set up the action for each shot and let it happen in front of the camera. This is not only quicker and easier to do but also gives the cutting room some control over the timing.

Technique is important in films but ultimately what matters is content. Complicated shots draw attention to themselves; they usually put technique before content. Keep it simple.

EDIT

    do you have the best shot and the best part?
    is it the right length?
    shorter is better
    don't cut unless you have to
    each shot should advance the action
    drop redundant shots
    make your team look good
    don't be hopeful
    don't cut during camera moves
    cut on action
    use sound to disguise a bad cut
    avoid parallel cuts
    don't cut between the same shot sizes
    two-shots can be a problem
    give montages some sort of visual sense
    check rhythm and pace of cuts
    don't let cuts become predictable
    the best cuts go unnoticed
    use mixes sparingly

List and view material

You have shot your film in ways that maximise your choices in the cutting room. Now is the time to take advantage of the opportunities you have won for yourself.

First of all, brief the editor. Tell him or her what the programme is trying to achieve, what the most important scenes are, the look you were trying for in the shooting and the style you are hoping for in the editing. Some directors give the editor the paperwork to read; others prefer to let the shots speak for themselves within the overall framework they have outlined. It's best to let the editor choose his own way of working.

It's important that the editor views all the material available before starting to cut. Sometimes editing has to start before the shooting is over but try and arrange your schedule so that you can be there with him for this viewing. The editor is your first viewer and his first reactions are important. His reactions will also be fresher than yours, as he hasn't been on the shoot. You too should come to the material with as fresh an eye as possible. Forget the problems you had getting the material—they are no longer relevant. All that matters now is what is on the screen. What have you captured on camera? What does it say? How can you use it?

Viewing all the material before you start editing gives you an overall feel for it and allows you to assess its strengths and weaknesses. If you view/edit sequence by sequence, you're building in the dark, laying brick on brick with no idea what the finished house will look like. If you haven't seen all the shots, how can you make the most of them?

Shot   Take

27/2

Slate number

It's easy to remember your shots as pictures, not so easy to remember where to find them. So make a shot list for each roll or cassette. All you need is a slate number or time code to tell you where the shot is, followed by a short description.

Hours Mins Secs Frames

19:59:52:11

Time code

The more material you have, the more elaborate your shot list should be. For a short magazine item you need only the number and a word or two to identify the picture. For a longer programme you will save editing time by making a more complete list before you go to the cutting room. This should include the first and last words spoken in each shot. For scripted drama you will find it helpful to have a shot list with notes about the continuity and you might also mark up the script with lines known as 'tramlines' to show what each shot covers. The more lines there are next to a particular line of script, the more ways you can cut it.

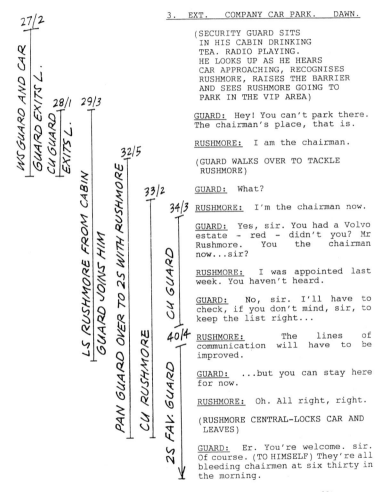

27/2

WS GUARD AND CAR

GUARD EXITS L.

28/1   29/3

CU GUARD EXITS L.

32/5

WS GUARD FROM CABIN

LS RUSHMORE FROM CABIN

GUARD JOINS HIM

PAN GUARD OVER TO 2S WITH RUSHMORE

33/2

CU RUSHMORE

34/3

CU GUARD

40/4

CU FAV. GUARD

2S

3.   EXT.   COMPANY CAR PARK.   DAWN.

(SECURITY GUARD SITS
IN HIS CABIN DRINKING
TEA. RADIO PLAYING.
HE LOOKS UP AS HE HEARS
CAR APPROACHING, RECOGNISES
RUSHMORE, RAISES THE BARRIER
AND SEES RUSHMORE GOING TO
PARK IN THE VIP AREA)

GUARD: Hey! You can't park there.
The chairman's place, that is.

RUSHMORE: I am the chairman.

(GUARD WALKS OVER TO TACKLE
RUSHMORE)

GUARD: What?

RUSHMORE: I'm the chairman now.

GUARD: Yes, sir. You had a Volvo
estate - red - didn't you? Mr
Rushmore.   You   the   chairman
now...sir?

RUSHMORE: I was appointed last
week. You haven't heard.

GUARD: No, sir. I'll have to
check, if you don't mind, sir, to
keep the list right...

RUSHMORE: The lines of
communication will have to be
improved.

GUARD: ...but you can stay here
for now.

RUSHMORE: Oh. All right, right.

(RUSHMORE CENTRAL-LOCKS CAR AND
LEAVES)

GUARD: Er. You're welcome. sir.
Of course. (TO HIMSELF) They're all
bleeding chairmen at six thirty in
the morning.

Don't forget to give the editor a copy of whatever type of list you make. Both of you can then use your lists to note the best shots and takes—the raw material for the first assembly of the film.

To get to that stage, you need a cutting order.

Do a cutting order

The cutting order is a 'paper edit'—a list for the editor of the shots you think worth including, in the order that you think will best tell the story. It should not be too tight; you will get a better film if you include all the usable shots to see how they work and then reduce them later. Make sure the cutting order is based on the shots you have, not the shots you hoped for. So don't be frightened to depart from the order in your original treatment, if the shots dictate it. The shots you planned for the opening, for example, may turn out to be a bit boring, so look for something that has more impact.

Don't forget sound when you are doing the cutting order; it needs planning and thinking about as much as the pictures. It's worth noting the sources on your order: sync sound, music, effects, narration or commentary, interview used as voice-over. You can then check that you have allowed for some variety, as too much from a single source can sound monotonous. The most common mistake is to have narration followed by interview followed by narration followed by interview followed by narration followed by... in other words, an unbroken torrent of words from start to finish. Leave room for the film to 'breathe' and for the viewers to catch their breath. The sound of a door opening or a car driving off, left clear without narration, can give rhythm and shape to a film as effectively as full stops and commas give rhythm and shape to words.

Work out which shots to write over and which shots to keep free. Some shots—trains thundering past camera, guns going off, buildings collapsing—are too strong to take narration; the pictures drown the words and viewers will miss whatever you are trying to tell them. Other shots - general views, long shots, people reading or driving—demand narration and often cannot keep their place in the film without it.

Why not write the narration first and then cut the pictures to it? The trouble with this approach is that it lures you into telling your story with words rather than pictures. So you miss touches like the door opening or the car driving off and destroy the effect of the train thundering past by suppressing the sound and putting narration over it. None of these shots looks impressive on paper—(X enters) or (car drives off) or (train passes). On the screen, however, such incidents not only offer relief from the torrent of words, they also add to your story. The way X enters —confidently or hesitantly or whatever—can communicate volumes to the viewers; the train passing can say 'urgent' or 'modern' or 'decrepit and undercapitalised' far more effectively than words.

The earlier the narration is written, the more intrusive it is. If you write it before editing, you limit what the editor can do with the shots. The words lead; the editor has to do what he or she can to get the pictures to follow. If you write the narration even earlier, before shooting, the tendency is to look for shots to cover the words rather than shots that tell the story (see the next two pages). Talking about things happening (in narration, interviews or pieces to camera) is easier than showing things happening. But it's far less effective for the viewers.

The ideal, of course, is this. First, make as much of your story as possible happen in front of the camera; then cut the pictures and sound to tell as much of the story as possible; and then write narration for those bits of the story that it can handle most economically and powerfully. If you have to make minor adjustments to some of the shots so that they fit the narration, fair enough. It's only when words do all the driving that pictures become passengers.

Check the first assembly

The cutting order leads to the first assembly. If you are using video, this stage is often called the off-line edit, as it's done on cheaper, non-broadcast-quality, off-line machines; the final cut will be done on expensive, broadcast-quality, on-line machines. If you are using film, the first assembly is often called the rough cut.

The first assembly is important because it's the first time that you and the editor can see how well the material works when cut together. The effect of shots on each other is not always predictable. In the cutting order shot A followed by shot B may seem a good idea; on screen it turns out that A swamps B or

If you write the words before shooting, you tend to look for shots to cover the words

"THESE TREES ARE ALREADY DEAD...."

"THE RANGERS ARE TAKING THE EMPTY NEST BOXES DOWN."

"TESTING SHOWS THAT THE WATER IS GETTING WORSE **EVERY** YEAR."

SPOKESPERSON –
"WE'RE WORKING ON THE THEORY THAT IT'S THE POWER STATIONS IN THE SOUTH."

"THE COLD HAS STRIPPED THE NORTH BARE OF TREES. IT LOOKS LIKE POLLUTION WILL DO THE SAME IN THE SOUTH."

Let pictures lead

makes B irrelevant or is itself irrelevant when followed by B. Or both shots are more effective if their order is reversed: B A.

The same is true of sequences.

Go through the first assembly, assessing how well each bit works. Are the shots and sequences in the right order? How well do they tell the story? Do you need all of them? Is the structure right? Is it too predictable? Are there any surprises? How can it be improved?

The first assembly is an exciting stage in programme-making. Till now there has been no film, only ideas, plans, shots and sounds for a film. Now there is a film, a living, moving thing that exists in time and takes on a life and shape of its own. And you created it...

The next stage is to make it better. This will inevitably involve changes. If you are editing film, there's no problem because you can trim shots, swap them round or drop them by physically cutting the stock. Video presents more of a problem because you can't physically cut the tape. When you shorten a shot, you don't shorten the tape—you just use less of it. So you can't go back to make changes on a video; you can only work forwards. This discourages experiment but in practice it's not too much of a drawback. If you have a programme that needs a lot of swapping around of shots and sequences, it's worth breaking it down into two or three sections at the off-line stage and editing each section on separate cassettes. If you foresee a really difficult edit, you can transfer all your material to film and edit on film. Some people prefer this anyway.

Work on details

When you have a first assembly, you are about half way through the editing. You have reviewed the overall shape and thrust; now is the time to get down to details.

Look at each shot and make sure it's *the best shot* and *the best part of the shot* to tell your story.

Look at each shot and make sure it's *the right length*. Does it come and go too quickly? Or does it outstay its welcome? The more detailed and interesting a shot is, the longer you can keep it on screen. If its neighbours deal with the same scene, the viewers will get the message faster and you can cut the shot tighter; if the shot is the only one dealing with the scene, it probably needs to be on screen longer. Judging how long a shot should be on screen is difficult: you have to 'feel' it. But there is an ideal length and when it looks right and feels right, it probably is right. Keep each shot on screen for the length of time it holds the attention, and not a moment longer.

You will find that these decisions about length give you the most agonies; your judgement suffers as you become more familiar—perhaps over-familiar—with the material and as you tire. But there's a good general rule for editing: *shorter is better*. If in doubt, cut it out.

On the other hand, *don't cut unless you have to*. Some shots can stay on screen for 30 seconds or more because they cover the action and hold the viewers' interest. There's no point cutting to shot B if it adds nothing to what viewers already know from shot A. You don't have to use all the shots you have of a particular action: *each shot should advance the action*.

Drop redundant shots. They slow things down and weaken the drive of the story. Be kind to your performers and cameraman and leave out shots that didn't go well for them—don't just put the shots in anyway and say 'It's not my fault the performance is bad' or 'It's not my fault the focus is soft'. It's your job to *make your team look good*.

And *don't be hopeful*; if you aren't sure that a shot works, it almost certainly won't work for the viewers.

If a shot is a developing shot (the camera moves to follow the action), you need to keep it on screen till the end of the camera move. Cutting during a zoom, pan or track rarely looks good. So *don't cut during camera moves*. Sometimes, however, a cut to another zoom, pan or track moving at exactly the same speed does work.

If you have overlapping shots, *cut on the action*. So if you have a long shot of someone walking to a chair and then sitting down followed by a closer shot of the same action, cut at the point where the person drops into the chair. The action will draw attention away from the cut. If the editor cuts out a few frames from the centre of the movement so that the sitting down is faster on screen than in real life, the transition between the two shots will be even smoother.

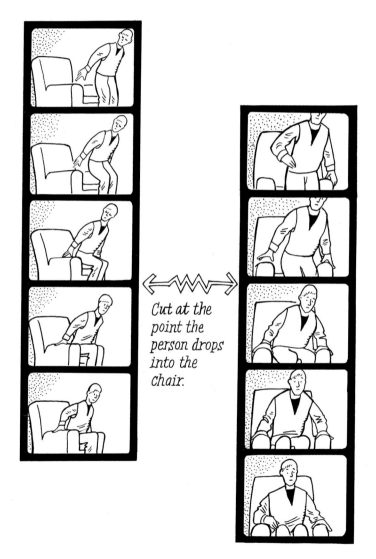

Cut at the point the person drops into the chair.

A *distinctive sound* such as a door slamming or zip being opened can also offer a good cutting point. If the continuity on your overlapping shots is not quite right, cutting on sound and/or action will go a long way towards hiding the mistake. If viewers have a lot to take in at the same time (action, sound and shot change), they won't be watching continuity. If you make the distinctive sound loud enough, viewers will probably blink and miss the cut altogether.

Your cuts will also be less obtrusive if you *avoid parallel cuts*—in other words, don't cut picture and sound at exactly the same point.

If the sound transition comes a little before or after the picture cut, the edit will look and sound smoother.

Don't cut between the same-sized shots of the same thing, if it makes the cut jump. If there is a change of angle between the two shots, the cut may work; the bigger the change of angle between the two shots, the more likely the cut will work. So cutting between two close-ups of the same person looks awful if there is only a small change of angle; on the other hand, it can be acceptable if you go from a front shot to a more profile shot of the same size. The cut will be even better, though, if the more profile shot is a different size.

Cutting between *two-shots* of people talking to each other is often a problem because the conversing couple jump across the screen as you favour first one speaker, then the other. The cuts will work if the shots match each other precisely, both in size and angle. But continuity can still be a problem, as it should be right for both actors on both sides of the cut; in practice the cut usually works if the continuity is right for the person the viewers look at in the incoming shot. The way to avoid being caught out by these difficulties is to make sure that you cover the conversation with single shots of the speakers as well.

Cutting between *two shots of a static object* is always difficult as there is no action to disguise the cut. The best way to make this type of cut work is to make sure there is a big change in size and angle between the two shots.

If you have a *montage of shots* —for example, of tourists looking round a cathedral—don't just put the shots in at random; try and find an order that makes some sort of visual sense. Perhaps follow shots of people who are very interested in the architecture, tombs and so on with shots of people and children who are not; or contrast the crowded cathedral shop with people ignoring the collection boxes.

Keep an eye on the *rhythm and pace* of cuts as these give your programme style. You need to step back every now and then and check the overall effect by running some of your cut sequences without stopping. This viewing will also highlight cuts that aren't quite right. Don't be frightened to make minute adjustments: a few frames longer or shorter can make a lot of difference.

On the other hand, *don't let cuts become predictable.* If the rhythm and pace never change and there are no surprises, your film can become monotonous. You have to keep a jump or two ahead of the viewers.

The best cuts in a film go unnoticed, because they are smooth and bring new information to the screen precisely when the viewers want it. Bad cuts, on the other hand, draw attention to themselves. They jump. Or (like the punctuation of this sentence) they, are out—of place.

This is the problem with *cross-fades, dissolves or mixes*: they draw attention to themselves. Of course, they work perfectly well as a transition between scenes or to denote the passing of time, though these uses are perhaps a little old-fashioned. They work best of all when you want to contrast two objects or details that are in exactly the same part of the screen. But as a regular device to get from one shot to another, mixes take longer than cuts and are more obtrusive. They also make life more difficult for any future programme-maker who wants to use your shots as archive material: it's difficult to find a clean in-point and a clean out-point in footage that is covered with mixes.

Films are made in the cutting room

Editing repays effort. It also takes time: for a short film at least twice the time it took to shoot, for a long film perhaps three times longer than the shoot—or more. (For those working with video, editing time includes the off-line, where you should do as much as possible of the detailed work mentioned above.)

Why does it take so long?

Firstly, because there are a lot of cuts to do. Most films have six to ten cuts per minute; assuming eight cuts a minute, a half-hour programme will have more than 200 cuts in it. Separate edits for sound may notch up another 50 cuts. The techniques and technology for finding shots get faster all the time, but 250 cuts is still a lot of work.

Secondly, how many cuts will you get right first time? The success rate improves with experience, but it's never 100 per cent. Editing is an art rather than a science.

And thirdly, your thinking develops as you work through the programme: you see new ways of juxtaposing the material, short cuts and better ways of telling the story. If you could speed up this development, find good solutions without having to go through bad—in fact, if you could get from A to C without having to go through B, editing would be a lot quicker.

Of course, you can't cut it if you haven't shot it. Editing will inevitably expose gaps in your material: key shots—perhaps a whole sequence—that are missing. If you are doing a long film, it can be helpful to keep one shooting day in hand to fill in the gaps. In practice, however, don't rely too much on your day in hand. It can work well to produce chapter headings or a series of pieces to camera (if that is the style of film you are doing). But as a way of eking out deficient sequences, it will be less successful. How many locations can you get back to in a day? Will your performers still be available, willing to help, and looking the same (a haircut can ruin continuity)? When you start to think about going back, the problems appear.

There are three other ways of trying to deal with gaps. Graphics are good at condensing information and presenting it attractively, but you have to be lucky for this solution to fit your problem. Video effects can manipulate your pictures in a bewildering number of ways but the manipulation only works if you have good strong material to start with; if you don't, no amount of visual razzmatazz will hide it. The third way of dealing with gaps—often the best, if you can get away with it— is to leave them unfilled. Viewers are usually more critical of what is put in than what is left out.

Finally, how long should you spend with the editor? This depends on you and the editor but if films are made in the cutting room, it seems sensible that you should be there. If you spend long periods away from the cutting room, your thinking about the shots and the way they go together doesn't develop and your ideas stay stuck at the cutting order stage. You then have to go along with the editor's decisions or perhaps ask him to try out your original idea, which you think he didn't understand but he knows didn't work ... all of which wastes time. The cutting room is the place where your deficiencies as a director become most apparent. So it's the best place to learn from your mistakes.

The other argument for staying in the cutting room becomes clear when you are in it: editing is immensely satisfying and creative. For many people it's the most enjoyable part of making programmes.

INTERVIEWS

Go for opinion, experience, anecdote rather than facts

Don't despise the talking head. It's the most interesting thing on television; it can also be the most boring. It appears the easiest thing to do; it can be the most difficult. Produced well, a talking head seems wholly natural—the art that makes it work conceals itself. But in fact a good interview is a performance. Only if it goes wrong do you realise that what appears natural is in fact artificial.

The point of an interview is to get first-hand comment. You want it straight from the horse's mouth: the personal opinions, experiences, anecdotes that only the interviewee can give you. Too many questions about undisputed facts and the interviewer begins to sound like a quizmaster: 'What year was the United Nations set up? Where are its headquarters? Who was the founder?' If these are important facts, they should have been in the introduction to the interview. Your interviewee must have more interesting things to say about the early days of the UN. He should also have stories to tell, because stories are what viewers remember. If he/she hasn't, you shouldn't be interviewing him/her.

Do a run-through

The run-through is a session before the recording or broadcast for the interviewer and interviewee to discuss what they are going to talk about. You should attend the run-through even if you have a specialist interviewer or reporter on the production: you're the one who has to fit the interview into the rest of the programme. Also, two heads are often better than one when you are trying to get the best out of an interviewee.

The run-through is not a rehearsal. If you give the interviewee all the questions and he gives you all the answers, the interview proper will be a repeat and will look and sound like one. If you are really unlucky, the interviewee will keep on saying 'As I was saying earlier...' or 'As I told you before...' to remind you that he is aware that he is repeating himself. This doesn't help the illusion of spontaneity you are trying to create.

The run-through can be quite short. Map out the areas you want to talk about. Probe areas that might—or might not—be interesting to go into ('What would you say if I ask about...?'). Consider suggestions from the interviewee ('Do you want me to talk about...? Should I mention ...?'). If the interviewee tries to stake out no-go areas, concede peripheral land (you probably won't have time to explore it during the interview) but be firm about entering the heartland.

What happens if you don't have a run-through?

The interviewer doesn't know the best way to tackle the interviewee, so many of his questions fall flat. The interviewee doesn't know what the programme is about or what is expected of him and so can't give of his best. Both performers are uneasy and the interview isn't as good as it could be.

Treat questions as prompts (be challenging)

The interviewer shouldn't have to drag every word out of the interviewee, like a barrister cross-examining a reluctant witness. Ideally he or she should be able to use the questions as prompts, guiding the interviewee over the ground to be covered and making sure he doesn't stray. If you have prepared the ground well in the run-through, the interviewee should know what is wanted and will do his best to deliver. He wants the interview to be a success as much as you do.

The worst questions to ask are those which invite short or yes/no answers, particularly at the start of the interview.

'When did you go to New York?' 'Last Thursday.' 'How long did you stay?' 'Three days.' 'The court hearing was on Friday?' 'Yes.'

You will find that the questions getting short or yes/no answers are the fact-finding questions that you should have raised in the run-through; the answers contain the information that you should have put into the introduction to the interview. The interview itself should take the viewer beyond these preliminaries. It's best to think of yourself as representing the viewers at home, asking the straightforward down-to-earth questions they would ask. After researching a subject you often know so much that you forget the questions that the ordinary viewer would like answered.

How you ask the questions will depend on how you intend to use the interview. If you intend to cut out the questions and use the answers only, you're probably better off not asking questions at all. Use 'Tell me...' instead. 'Tell me what happened when you arrived at the UN.' 'Tell me what people hoped for from the new organisation.'

The advantage of 'Tell me...' is that it invites the interviewee to give a full answer; he can't say just 'yes' or 'no'. His answer is also more likely to have a start that makes sense when you cut out the question during editing: 'I remember, I got to New York on a Wednesday, and...' 'At the time World War Two was at its height, and...'

If you notice that the answer won't make sense without the question and the subject isn't clear from the context, don't be afraid to stop the interviewee and suggest he starts his answer again with whatever words you want. But don't interrupt unless you really have to. Both the answers above, for example, make sense without the question, even though they don't directly refer to the question.

Write out the first question in full

If you intend to keep your questions in the interview, tell the sound recordist, as it affects the choice of mikes. Then write out the first question in full and jot down only a short phrase for each of the others. This makes your questions sound more natural, as the way you put your questions will automatically reflect what went before, something they can't do if you write them out in full in advance. This technique also provides you with a good argument for resisting the demand to submit all your questions in writing before the interview. You may have to give in to this demand (it's usually made by VIPs) but often a list of the topics you intend to raise will satisfy the interviewee.

When asking the questions during the interview, make sure that you don't interrupt the interviewee and cut short his answers. Some interviewers have a habit of doing this, making their interviews difficult—and sometimes impossible—to edit, because the interviewee never has a chance to finish an answer and there's nowhere for the editor to get his scissors in.

One last trap to avoid. Don't be too kind to the interviewee. Interviews should be challenging, not because you are trying to provoke a punch-up but because people perform better when they have to justify themselves. Grovelling questions like 'You really have been exceedingly far-sighted in your handling of this problem, haven't you?' put the interviewee in an impossible position. Agreement sounds smug. Denial sounds false. A mixture of both ('Not really—it was a tremendous stroke of luck') sounds both smug and false at the same time. Whatever the reply, the interview grinds to a halt. A wise interviewee would ignore the question and talk about something else.

Don't be too kind to the interviewee

Don't be afraid to stop

Interviews are difficult to do well. If you don't get it right first time and the interview isn't live, don't be frightened to stop recording and redo a part or the whole of the interview again.

You have to use your judgement about how to play this card. When you start recording, you often find that an interviewee becomes tense and it helps him or her hugely to stop after a couple of exchanges and start again from the top. The relief of tension when you stop is almost tangible—it's as if the interviewee stops holding his breath. When you start again, the pressure is much less and you get a better interview. For this safety valve to work you must stop the camera: the relief is not nearly as great if the camera keeps running while the interviewer encourages the guest to relax.

At other times it's unnecessary to stop the camera. A pause is enough, for example, if you are doing the sort of interview where you intend to drop the questions and an answer doesn't start clearly enough to stand alone. You can also keep the camera running if you only want to change the size of shot or are interviewing several people at the same time.

Keep the interviewer near the camera

This is the golden rule for shooting an interview, both on location and in the studio.

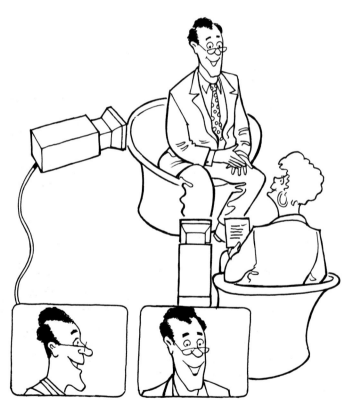

The greater the distance between interviewer and camera, the more profile the shot

The reason is simple. People tend to look at each other when they are talking, so if the interviewer is near the camera, the camera will have a full-face shot of the interviewee. One-eye profile shots are less satisfactory because they restrict the information that viewers get from the face. They can work as a variation to the full-face shot in a long interview, but if you are offering nothing but a profile shot viewers will feel deprived.

You often get a profile shot when there is only one camera and the interviewer decides to start with an introduction to camera. She looks directly at the camera, says her bit and turns to the interviewee. The camera zooms and pans to show the interviewee and bingo!—you have two speakers talking across the camera, the classic profile-producing situation. The golden rule has been broken: the interviewer isn't near the camera.

So how does the interviewer get from standing in front of the camera to near the camera? There are two ways. The first is for the interviewer to take a step towards the camera as she turns to look at the interviewee. This moves her to a position near the camera and so everything is as it should be. Taking a step while turning feels a bit odd at first, so the interviewer should practise a couple of times before shooting. This also gives the camera operator a chance to rehearse his part in the proceedings.

The second (and easier) way is to position the camera to one side so that it will have a full-face shot of the interviewee when the interviewer turns to face him after the introduction.

Position the camera to one side

I said at the start that staying near the camera is the golden rule for studio as well as location interviews. The only difference is that in the studio you have two cameras, so the technique is doubled: each performer stays near a camera (or—in practice—each camera stays near the line of looking). This gives you the 'cross-shooting' arrangement that is standard for studio interviews.

One final tip for shooting interviews: keep it simple. Directors often like to start an interview with a two-shot over the interviewer's shoulder, zoom in on the interviewee and then follow with regular changes in the size of the shot during the questions. With hindsight these movements usually turn out to be a bad idea, particularly for location interviews. They create more problems for the editor (cuts during camera moves don't look good) than they contribute to the picture.

Holding a good medium close-up—the bottom of the picture cutting just below the interviewee's armpits—is a far better bet. You can then shoot all your cutaways of the interviewer in medium close-up as well and know that they will always be the correct matching size.

Instead of introducing camera movements, concentrate on listening to the questions and answers to make sure that nothing vital is missed. Look and listen also for sections that might benefit from a retake.

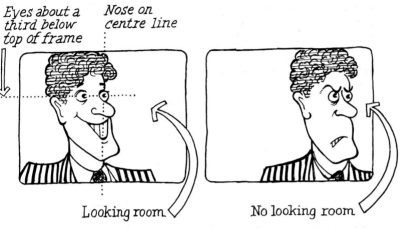

Eyes about a third below top of frame

Nose on centre line

Looking room

No looking room

And before you start shooting, make sure the composition of the shot is right.

Shoot cutaways (on another cassette)

Always shoot cutaways—for interviews as for the rest of your programme. If you don't need to use them, so much the better. If you do need to use them and don't have them, you have problems.

When shooting cutaways the aim is to fool the viewers into thinking you have two cameras for the interview. So the way to shoot them is to move the camera to where the second camera would be if you were cross-shooting in the studio (see illustration on page 74). The cutaways should match the shots of the interviewee in size, angle and eyeline—with the interviewer, of course, looking to the other side of camera. All this is easier if you use only one size of shot for the interviewee. If the cameraman changes size, you should do cutaways in two or more sizes to make sure you can match the shots of the interviewee.

If you have an assistant who can take down the questions as they are put, the interviewer can record the main ones as a cutaway, trying to reproduce the way he asked them as accurately as possible. Remembering and repeating the exact inflection is

SHOOTING INTERVIEW CUTAWAYS

Interviewee

Interviewer

4. Interviewer in shot sizes used for interview doing
(1) Cutaway questions.
(2) Reaction shots (noddies)

3. If interviewee has time,
OTS 2S. FAV. INT'R.
Int'ee talks
Int'r listens

1. Zoom out for over-the shoulder two-shot favouring interviewee (OTS 2S. FAV. INT'EE)
Int'ee listens, Int'r talks.

2. Wide two-shot.
So that you can't see lips move

difficult. One way round the problem is to record the questions during the interview on a second recorder (make sure the switch can't be heard on the interview track) and then play them back for the interviewer to repeat.

By the way, recording cutaway questions is one of the times you don't need to keep stopping the camera: let it run while the interviewer works through the list. Leave a couple of seconds of silence between questions so that you end up with a clean recording of all the questions you might need, plus a few listening shots or 'noddies'.

The problem with moving the camera to shoot cutaways is that it takes time—if you are using lights, you may have to wait for a complete re-rig. A quicker way is to put the interviewer in the interviewee's position and then move the chair and camera slightly so that there is a different background behind the interviewer. The lights then need only a small adjustment. The viewers will never know you have 'cheated'—unless you are also using wide two-shots for cutaways, which might give the game away.

Move chair and camera slightly to change background.

Interviewee looked camera left.

Interviewer must look camera right

You can speed up the editing of a long interview by shooting cutaways on another cassette. If the cutaways are on the same cassette as the interview, the editor has to waste time spooling through the interview to get to them. If the cutaways are on another cassette, it can be put in another machine and the editor can work through the interview and cutaways in parallel. You don't, of course, have this problem with film because you can go directly to each shot once the rushes have been broken down.

You will find it also saves editing time to use a clapper board when shooting video, even though the board isn't needed to synchronise picture and sound. The board provides a visual marker for the beginning of a shot or take, and so you don't have to keep referring to time codes during the edit. It is easy to spot when the tape is spooling through at speed. You don't waste any time putting it on the shot, because it can be put on during the run-up (there is no need to clap it). And many directors regard it as a useful discipline on location. When the board goes in front of the camera, everyone starts to concentrate.

Edit interviews first; then put in cutaways

The procedure for editing interviews differs slightly from that for editing other material.

When you are logging, make a note of the questions and where they are, using either time code or slate numbers. Put a tick next to any answers that are likely to be included in the cutting order. At this stage select the whole answer or chunks of it; it's easier to do the fine trimming later. Then look at the cutaways and the cutaway questions so that you know what is available.

If you have a transcript of the interviews, bracket off the best passages when viewing. Some people don't bother viewing interviews if they have transcripts and work from the paper only —a rather hit-and-miss approach, as it makes no allowance for the way the words are spoken.

When the editor does the first assembly, interview cuts are normally left as jump cuts without cutaways. If they were in at this stage you would have to take them out again (and perhaps re-dub part of the interview) each time you wanted to change a cut. The cutaways are put in only at the last stage of the edit, when there are unlikely to be any more changes. The only exception is questions that have been re-recorded for cutaways: these should be included in the first assembly as you can't assume they will be the same length as the ones asked during the interview. But be sparing in your use of cutaway questions; put them in because they are an improvement on the original, not just because you have them.

Finally, if you are using parts of the interview as voice-over (in other words, using the sound over shots of what the interviewee is talking about), you should make the sound flow as smoothly as possible by cutting out the hesitations, ums and ers. If the interviewee is not a good speaker, leave a few in to keep the voice-over section in character!

Understand the rules
(so you can break them)

Interviews have their own rules of behaviour, like any social activity. The rules aren't written down but interviewees are usually aware of them because they have watched television and seen how people behave. If they don't already know what is acceptable, they get the idea during the run-through; indeed, this is one of the (unspoken) reasons for the run-through.

Some rules. The interviewee agrees to be questioned, often on points he would prefer not to answer. The interviewer agrees not to press him too far. The interviewee agrees not to criticise the questions. The interviewer agrees not to criticise the answers. Both agree to steer clear of details that don't broadcast well. And so on.

The rules are informal and often difficult to define. You may become aware of them only when they are broken; when, for example, an inexperienced interviewee answers a question in too much detail. Or insists on giving a lecture instead of an answer. If the interviewee doesn't mend his ways, he or she is branded as a 'bad' interviewee and not invited again.

Sometimes watching the rules being broken is entertaining. An interviewer casts doubts on an interviewee's sincerity—more gentlemanly behaviour is the rule. A crew push their way into someone's home or office and try to hustle him into answering questions—interviews are usually by consent. An interviewee starts to ask questions instead of answering them; or challenges the interviewer's understanding of the subject ('You haven't read my report'); or doesn't like the direction the interview is taking and tries to change it. Sometimes consensus on the rules breaks down altogether and the interview collapses because the aims of both sides are so far apart. Such episodes—if they can be transmitted—are often called 'good' television.

Understanding the rules is important. Firstly, because the rules steer you round some of the pitfalls. And secondly, because understanding the rules gives you the confidence to bend or even break them. This could turn the ritual of the interview into something that makes your programme exceptional.

SHOOT FOR VIEWERS

What do you want them to see?

Don't make programmes for your eyes only—that's the province of some experimental 'art' directors. But do make programmes that you want to make and you yourself want to see. There's not much point doing it if your heart's not in it.

The danger with making programmes for your eyes only is that you forget to communicate with the viewer. You know the story already and so chunks of the plot or argument are left out and the programme dives into obscurity. The unfortunate viewers are soon floundering:

'Yes, yes. Very nice. But what's it about?'

The other extreme is making programmes that don't interest you at all but will (you think) interest the great public out there. This also is dangerous. The great public out there is made up of people like you. If you make a habit of dissociating yourself from your product, you may slowly lose touch with your audience. Your talent for 'knowing what people want' can become tainted, first with cynicism and then with contempt. You may become very rich (like the designers of some successful quiz shows) but your programmes lose their sincerity and freshness and become mechanical.

You have to strike a balance. Make programmes that interest you, but make them for the viewers, not for yourself.

So, what do you want them to see?

Up to now we have been discussing techniques for getting pictures and sound on to the screen to tell the story. Now we go to the other side of the screen and consider the pictures themselves and how we look at them. This will help us understand why some shots and cuts work better than others.

Pictures have many meanings

You rarely see pictures without words. Paintings have labels, postcards are identified on the back, newspaper photographs have captions. The reason is that pictures are ambiguous: they have more than one possible interpretation or meaning.

Pictures need words. Without words you don't know how to 'read' them. Imagine a photo of a woman with flowing hair sipping an iced drink on a palm-fringed tropical beach. Who is she? Where is she? What is she? Is she a holiday-maker? Is she a model? Is she advertising something? If she is, is it make-up, shampoo, hair-spray, perfume, swimwear, the iced drink, the tropical island, a travel company? Without words all these interpretations are possible and, of course, there are many more.

The extent of the ambiguity depends on your familiarity with the content. The more familiar the content, the less the ambiguity, and the less the need for words. If the woman in the picture is your sister and you show it to her, no explanation is needed. Your mother may require a few words of explanation: 'Lucy was trying the fruit cocktail' (Mother knows you went on holiday together). Your colleagues at work probably won't recognise your sister or the place (they know you were on holiday); they will need more words. A visitor from abroad won't know anything about the woman, the place or the holiday. A jungle tribesman might require explanation of woman, place, cocktail, beach, dress, even what holidays are.

Some pictures show things that are unmistakable (the Eiffel Tower, the Statue of Liberty, Mickey Mouse, children, animals) or communicate instantly recognisable concepts (love, sex, nature, beauty, divinity, peace, freedom). These pictures can do their job away from other pictures and without words because they are part of our culture and we read them in that context.

The narrower, immediate context also affects the ambiguity of pictures. If the photo of the woman is shown as one of a set of holiday snaps, it is easier to decide—and explain—what it is. It becomes less ambiguous.

In television and the cinema the pictures come in a stream and are never seen alone. So moving pictures are less ambiguous because they are always seen in the context of their companions. Our brains have a strong tendency to look for pattern and impose sense, even when we know the results are nonsense (looking for pictures in wallpaper stains, 'seeing' the man in the moon). If the photo of the woman appears in a sequence of shots of swimwear, it becomes part of a fashion show:

In a sequence showing bottles and a barman, it's part of a cocktail-making demonstration:

Surrounded by police photos, it's a clue in a cops and robbers show:

Juxtaposing pictures reduces their ambiguity. Reducing ambiguity is one of the aims of editing. A long shot can be read in many different ways. Follow it by a close-up and you eliminate many of the possible interpretations.

In fact most of what you do when you make a programme can be thought of in terms of reducing ambiguity. When you shoot, you use action, lighting, angle, shot size and camera movement to reduce the ambiguity—if pictures weren't ambiguous, you would shoot everything in long shot. When you edit, you should assemble the pictures to make as much sense as possible and when you have told as much of the story as you can with pictures, you drive the message home with sound. Sound is the television equivalent of the label on the painting, the postcard identification and the newspaper caption.

Eyes look at one part of the screen at a time

It may seem strange to talk about looking at a part of the screen. Isn't the screen small enough for our eyes to take in the whole picture at once?

It is, but that isn't the way eyes work.

Eyes focus on one point of interest at a time; then they move to another point of interest, then to another, then perhaps back to the first. The period at rest can be very brief; it depends what there is to look at. The moves are always very fast; in fact, unless they are following an object, eyes can't do a slow, steady pan—they dart. The scene around each point of interest is out of focus and in peripheral vision (which simply means, to the side).

Eyes go to light

One consequence of this system of sudden jumps (known as saccades) is that there is a rough order for seeing things. Eyes go to the light part of the scene first, which is why the spotlight picks out the star and the car with the sidelights on is the one you see first.

Eyes also go to movement; they can't help it. This is probably a primitive, animal reflex, as movement— particularly sudden movement—represents potential danger. So if something stirs in the undergrowth, you look; if people want to be seen, they wave. Conjurors have traded on this for years: if they want to do something without people seeing, they make sure there is some other business going on

Eyes go to movement

to catch the eye. It's also perhaps the most fundamental reason for the success of television: if the set is on, it's an effort not to look at it.

Unfortunately the eye going to movement is not always helpful for the programme-maker. If there is a fly on the interviewee's jacket, everyone watches the fly. If the busy newsroom is used as a background for the news, the room is more eye-catching than the reader. Neither problem is easy to fix. Fly-swatting is fun for viewers to watch but doesn't improve the interview. Banishing people (and therefore movement) from the newsroom while it is on air makes a nonsense of the setting: if it isn't busy, it isn't impressive.

Why does the busy office work better as a backdrop for drama than for news?

There will be many reasons, if the director knows his stuff. The background will be designed to complement the main action without setting up competing points of interest. The shot sizes and camera angles will be more adventurous than the news can be. The main actors will move and gesture—news anchors are by definition more static. The lighting will favour the main actors and the scene will be shot in such a way that the background is slightly out of focus. Watch a busy opening scene in a well-directed film and work out how the director makes you look at the main action.

Lights can also work against the programme-maker, particularly if they flash on and off. Pity the artist who has to dance or sing in a setting blazing with neon tubes and disco effects. If you want the star to be brighter than the firmament, be sparing with the wide shots or tone down the setting and make sure the star has a good spotlight.

Finally, the fact that eyes look at one part of the screen at a time gives you a way of checking that your cuts are smooth. If the point of interest in the outgoing shot is in the same position on the screen as the point of interest in the incoming shot, the cut will look smooth. This is how blatant jump cuts can be made to work. One moment your hero is jogging through the park; the next he's in the shower. If he's in the same part of the screen in both shots, the cut will usually work.

SHOOT FOR VIEWERS

Eyes select; people see things differently

Vision is selective. Eyes and brain working together choose what to see and what not to see.

The power of this ability is a little frightening. Think how efficiently the nose is left out of your picture of the world; your brain knows you aren't interested (except when you're thinking about it, as now) and so your nose is rubbed out, without even a blank space left to mark its absence. Optical illusions, hallucinations, mirages—your brain can make you 'see' things that aren't there. Even when your eyes are shut—think of dreams. It makes you wonder who is in control. Do eyes and brain play other tricks we don't know about?

Vision is all brain-work. It's an interpretive process, that has nothing to do with cameras, screens or mirrors. The eyes can be thought of as a visible part of the brain; in fact, part of the processing of visual inputs takes place in the retina at the back of the eye.

Almost all our personal attributes affect the way we see things. Sex: men and women tend to see different things in (say) cars, clothes, football, home furnishings—and each other. Age: policemen aren't getting younger every year; it's you and your idea of youth that are getting older. Education: study can be an eye-opener—take a walk with a geologist, botanist or zoologist and see the world as rocks, plants or habitat. Training: think of detectives deciphering clues, fortune-tellers reading palms, air traffic controllers monitoring radar screens. Job: cameramen look at light; hairdressers look at hair—and may remember it better than they remember the face. Spare-time chore: when you're painting, you see brush strokes; when you aren't, you don't. Emotional state: love lends you rose-coloured glasses; so does alcohol. And so on.

The result of all this is that people see things differently. The lesson to draw for making programmes is to recognise that selective vision affects you too, both because of your personal attributes and because the programme-making process itself changes the way you look at the programme. By the time it is finished, there can be a great gap between the way you see the material and the way the viewers see the material. If you don't realise there is a gap and don't help the viewer bridge it, your programme can fail completely.

You get your first chance to see how far your eye has diverged from the norm when you look through the material with your first viewer, the editor. If he or she sees the shots differently from you, he or she is almost certainly right. The reactions of superiors, sponsors and clients are also helpful, provided they haven't been too involved in the production process.

Selective vision explains, I think, the great disasters of film and television. They start out as great projects, so they take a long time to make. The producers spend years on the project, so they forget what it looks like to the person in the street. Management and sponsors involve themselves in every detail (prestigious projects must have top-level supervision), so their judgement is compromised. As there is a huge budget, the picture editors often attend the shoot, so even their view of the material is not as fresh as it might be. Everyone is up to their necks in the project; there's no one left who can see and say, 'This doesn't work'.

On a more mundane level, selective vision often makes you miss things like equipment cases, tripods, reflections, throwaway cups, light stands and cables in the background of shots. You are so busy with the action and the actors that your eyes and brain ignore the debris.

Train yourself to check for foreign bodies before each shot. Cameras can't select.

The camera can't select (you have to help it)

The camera unblinkingly records everything in front of the lens, mirroring rather than selecting. The systematic way it scans a picture—line by line at split-second speeds—often produces pictures that don't look a bit like what we see with our eyes. This is why people react so strongly to shots of themselves: it's not the way they see themselves in the mirror.

For programme-makers the problem is to see shots as the camera does. It's a knack you acquire with experience but it is always helpful to look through the viewfinder (ask the cameraman first). Or—even better—take a monitor on location.

You can also look through half-closed eyes. This shows you how the scene will look on screen, as it reduces your ability to handle contrasting levels of light to roughly that of the camera. The gunman lurking motionless in the shade of the trees, easy to see when your eyes are wide open, will probably disappear altogether when they are half-closed. The camera probably won't see him either unless you help it. (Some suggestions: expose for the shade and accept that the sunlit parts of the shot will be overexposed; ask the gunman to put on a lighter jacket; put more light on him; ask him to scratch his nose; ask him to cough.)

The camera probably won't see the gunman

But why do shots look different? Why don't our eyes interpret the picture on the screen in the same way that they interpret the real world? Why can't we see ourselves on screen as we see ourselves in the mirror?

Part of the answer lies with the camera and its way of working, which is so different from the way our eyes work. It scans rather than saccades; it's weaker on contrast; it has only one lens (we have two eyes); it squeezes three dimensions into two. It's not surprising that the images it produces are different.

Part of the answer lies with the screen itself. It's always there when we view and its presence inevitably changes the way we see the picture. The most important effect is the way it reduces depth. You can fight this flattening effect and help restore the third dimension by emphasising features that suggest depth. Like shadows—don't shoot landscapes at midday when the shadows are shortest. Or by introducing 'dingle'—a plant or branch in the foreground that makes the brain see the rest of the picture as background.

Dingle

The effect of camera and screen on the way we see pictures is unpredictable. They seem to inhibit our selective vision—but not always. Some illusions fall away. The flattering image of ourselves that we see in the mirror gives way to the franker portrait on the screen. The equipment cases, tripods and throwaway cups that we overlooked during the shoot refuse to be overlooked in the shot. On the other hand, some illusions persist. We often continue to see merit in shots that have no merit, and perhaps fail to see the merit in shots that were done as an afterthought and yet say it all.

A last point about the camera and selectivity. The camera can't select, but you should be aware of how much selecting you do for it. You go to a location, look round and see all there is to see. Then you select part of what goes on there for the camera to record. You then record only selected bits of that action because you break it into shots; and the camera records only a small part of each setup because its angle of vision is narrower. All you take back to the cutting room is a tiny selection of pictures—which you then proceed to prune still further. It's easy to forget how much selecting you do for the camera and how selective the result is.

SHOOT FOR VIEWERS

It's not what you see that matters— it's what you make others see

Producers sometimes claim that they don't do any selecting at all: 'I don't need an angle; I just show it like it is'.

They are kidding themselves. The truth is that reality takes too long to put on screen. A dance group creating a musical, or the work of a rat-catcher may be interesting, but does the viewer really want to live through every minute? Of course not. Producers are forced to make choices about what to shoot and what to leave out. They also don't have unlimited stock, and so they stop shooting during the boring bits like coffee breaks. The trouble is, the most interesting things often happen during the boring bits like coffee breaks.

The debris refuses to be overlooked on camera

Notice also the programme-maker has to say 'I just tell it like it is'. He has to take a personal, subjective view of his story; he can't be objective, because he is an individual. The camera can't be objective either. Someone has to operate it and operating it involves choice, choosing where to put it and which way to point it and when to start and stop it and what to leave out as the action develops.

What the programme-maker aims for is not reality, but the illusion of reality. It's a difficult trick to pull off. The dance group plan and rehearse their musical for weeks, the rat-catcher has a lifetime of experience—and you have to condense all that reality into a few minutes. Not only does reality take too long to put on the screen, it's frequently also the wrong shape and size, poorly lit and happening over too wide an area for camera and mike to capture successfully (I'm thinking of the problems of shooting a dance rehearsal with six dancers, a choreographer and a piano in a large and gloomy rehearsal room). You have to use all your programme-making skills to make it look real on screen because the only reality communicated by poor shooting is poor shooting.

In the end directing video and film is selecting your version of reality and putting it on the screen. To paraphrase Degas, the Impressionist artist: it's not what you see that matters—it's what you make others see.*

---

* Degas is quoted in *La Renaissance de l'art français* (1918) as saying 'The artist does not draw what he sees, but what he has to make others see'.

INDEX